PIANO • VOCAL • GUITAR

ULTIMATE

GOSPEL DISCARDED

D0886155

◆ 100 SONGS 100 OF DEVO

ISBN 0-7935-4594-3

HAL•LEONARD
CORPORATION

7777 W. BLUEMOUND RD. P.O. BOX 13819 MILWAUKEE, WI 53213

PIANO • VOCAL • GUITAR
ULTIMATE Gospel

• 100 SONGS OF DEVOTION •

AMAZING GRACE

Words and Music by
JOHN NEWTON

Verse 3
And when this flesh and heart shall fail
and mortal life shall cease.
I shall possess within the veil
a life of joy and peace.

When we've been there ten thousand years,
bright shining as the sun.

We've no less days to sing God's praise
than when we first begun.

BECAUSE HE LIVES

Words by WILLIAM J. and GLORIA GAITHER
Music by WILLIAM J. GAITHER

Not too slow

Verse

God sent His Son, _____ they called him Je- sus; _____
hold _____ our new- born ba- by, _____

_____ He came to love, _____ heal and for-
_____ And feel the pride _____ and joy He

give; _____ He lived and died _____
gives; _____ But great- er still _____

3. And then one day I'll cross that river;
   I'll fight life's final war with pain;
   And then as death gives way to vict'ry,
   I'll see the lights of glory and I'll know He reigns.

THE BLOOD WILL NEVER LOSE ITS POWER

Words and Music by
ANDRAÉ CROUCH

Moderately

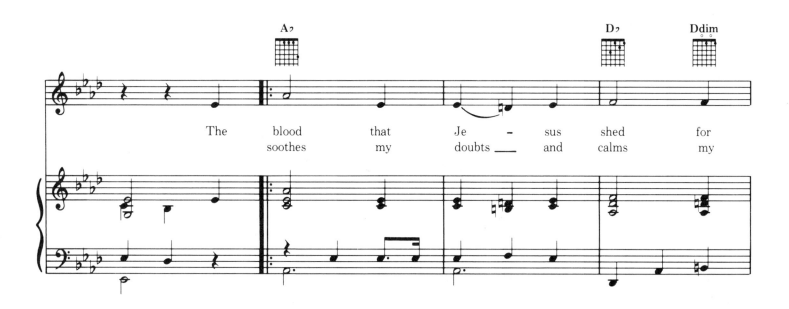

The blood that Je - sus shed for
soothes my doubts ___ and calms my

me,
fears,

Way back on Cal - va -
And it dries all my

BRIGHTEN THE CORNER WHERE YOU ARE

Words by INA DULEY OGDON
Music by CHARLES H. GABRIEL

Brightly

Do not wait un-til some deed of great-ness you may do, do not wait to send your light a-far, to the man-y du-ties ev-er near you now be true, bright-en the cor-ner

all your tal-ent you may sure-ly you find a need, here re-flect the Bright and Morn-ing Star, e-ven from your hum-ble hand the bread of life may feed, bright-en the cor-ner

CALVARY COVERS IT ALL

By MRS. WALTER G. TAYLOR

CLIMB EV'RY MOUNTAIN
from THE SOUND OF MUSIC

Lyrics by OSCAR HAMMERSTEIN II
Music by RICHARD RODGERS

COME MORNING

By DEE GASKIN

God's chil-dren ___ too long have ___ been bur-dened, ___
times I'm ___ de - spised and ___ re - ject - ed, ___

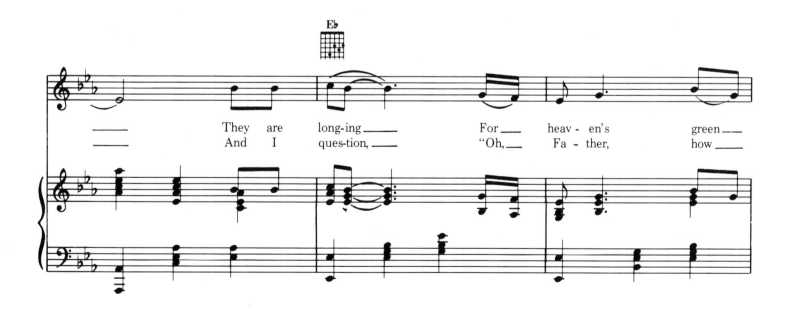

They are long-ing ___ For ___ heav-en's green ___
And I ques-tion, ___ "Oh, ___ Fa - ther, how ___

DADDY SANG BASS

Words and Music by
CARL PERKINS

help a trou - bled soul. _____ One of these

days and it won't be long, I'll re - join them in a

song; I'm gon - na join the fam - 'ly cir - cle at the

throne. _____ No, the cir - cle _____ won't be

DAY BY DAY
from the Musical GODSPELL

Words and Music by
STEPHEN SCHWARTZ

HE

Words by RICHARD MULLEN
Music by JACK RICHARDS

EL SHADDAI

Words and Music by MICHAEL CARD
and JOHN THOMPSON

In two, with much expression

El - Shad - dai,_____ El - Shad - dai,_ El - El - yon_ __ na A - do - nai,_____ age to age_____ you're still____ the same,_

EVERYTHING IS BEAUTIFUL

Words and Music by
RAY STEVENS

With movement

Je - sus loves the lit - tle

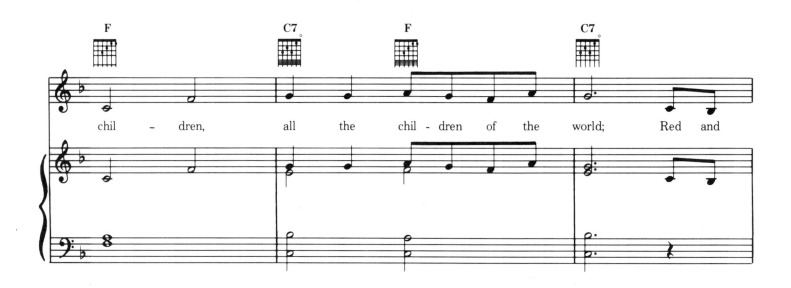

chil - dren, all the chil - dren of the world; Red and

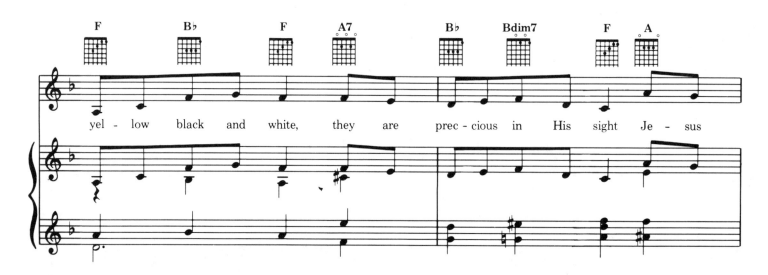

yel - low black and white, they are prec - cious in His sight Je - sus

39

THE FAMILY OF GOD

Words by WILLIAM J. and GLORIA GAITHER
Music by WILLIAM J. GAITHER

FILL MY CUP, LORD

By RICHARD BLANCHARD

3. So, my brother, if the things this world gave you
   Leave hungers that won't pass away,
   My blessed Lord will come and save you
   If you kneel to Him and humbly pray.

FINALLY

Words and Music by GARY CHAPMAN

46

FOR LOVING ME

Words and Music by
AARON WILBURN

50

FOR THE LOVE OF IT

Words and Music by JERRY MICHAEL
and KATHLEEN MURDOCK

HE GREW THE TREE

By CHUCK LAWRENCE

55

56

2. With tears in His eyes, God looked down through time;
   Saw Him spat upon, rejected and mocked.
   Still He grew the tree that He knew would be used
   to make an old rugged cross.

HE LOOKED BEYOND MY FAULT

Words and Music by
DOTTIE RAMBO

HE LIVES

By A.H. ACKLEY

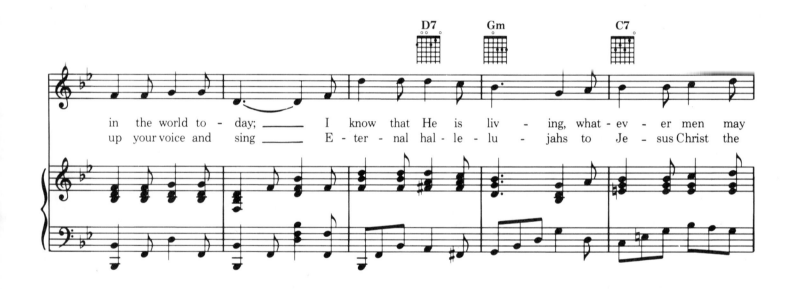

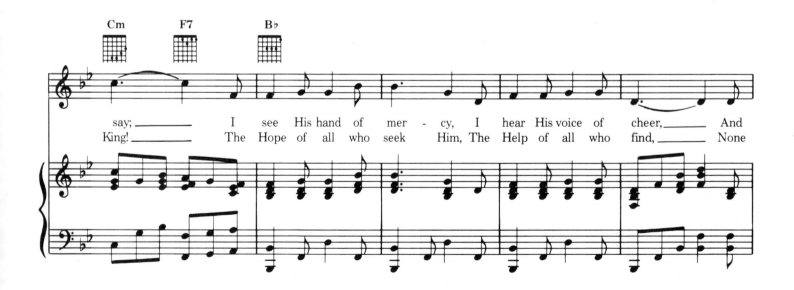

HE TOUCHED ME

Words and Music by
WILLIAM J. GAITHER

With an easy flow

C7 **C6** **C9** **F** **F♯dim** **C6** **C7**

Shack - led by a heav - y bur - den _____ 'Neath a load of
Since I met this bless - ed Sav - ior _____ Since He cleansed and

C6 **C7** **E7** **Fmaj7** **F6** **F7** **B♭maj7** **B♭6** **B♭** **Bdim**

guilt and shame _____ Then the hand of Je - sus
made me whole _____ I will nev - er cease to

F **Fmaj7** **F6** **F♯dim** **C6** **C7** **Gm7** **C6** **C7** **F**

touched me _____ and now I am no long - er the same. _____
praise Him _____ I'll shout it while e - ter - ni - ty rolls. _____

© Copyright 1963 by William J. Gaither
Copyright Renewed
All Rights Reserved Used by Permission

HE'S ALIVE

By DON FRANCISCO

6. Suddenly the air was filled with strange and sweet perfume;
   Light that came from ev'rywhere drove shadows from the room
   Jesus stood before me with his arms held open wide;
   And I fell down on my knees, And just clung to Him and cried.

7. He raised me to my feet and as I looked into His eyes,
   Love was shining out from Him like sunlight from the skies;
   Guilt and confusion disappeared in sweet release,
   Ev'ry fear I'd ever had just melted into peace.

HE'S EVERYTHING TO ME

Words and Music by
RALPH CARMICHAEL

In the stars His hand - i -
I will cel - e - brate Na -

work I see,
ti - vi - ty,

On the wind He speaks with maj - es - ty.
for it has a place in his - to - ry.

Though He rul - eth o - ver land and sea,
Sure, He came to set His peo - ple free;

what is that to
what is that to

HE'S GOT THE WHOLE WORLD IN HIS HAND

Traditional Spiritual

With spirit

3. He's got the whole church in His hand.
He's got the whole church in His hand.
He's got the whole church in His hand.
He's got the whole world in His hand.

4. He's got the whole world in His hand.
He's got the whole world in His hand.
He's got the whole world in His hand.
He's got the whole world in His hand.

HE'S STILL WORKIN' ON ME

By JOEL HEMPHILL

He's still work-in' on me to make me what I ought to be. It took Him just a week to make the moon and stars, the sun and the earth and Jup-i-ter and Mars. How lov-ing and pa-tient He must

HEY JESUS, YOU'RE MY BEST FRIEND

By MARY ANN KENNEDY
and DON GOODMAN

2. (You're the) only one I've ever found who didn't give up when I let 'em down:
   I guess that's how love's supposed to be.
   When there's no one else around,
   I fall down to the ground,
   I feel so tall down on my knees.
   (To Chorus)

HIS EYE IS ON THE SPARROW

Text by C.D.MARTIN
Music by CHARLES H. GABRIEL

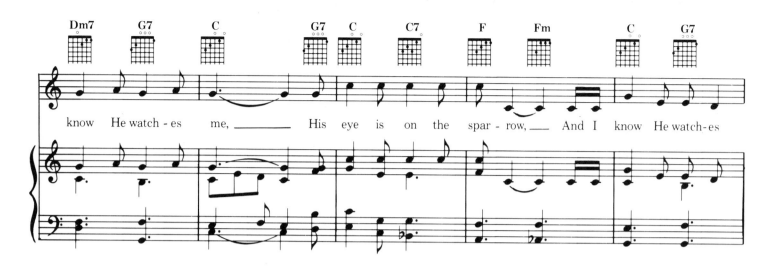

know He watch-es me, _____ His eye is on the spar - row, ___ And I know He watch-es

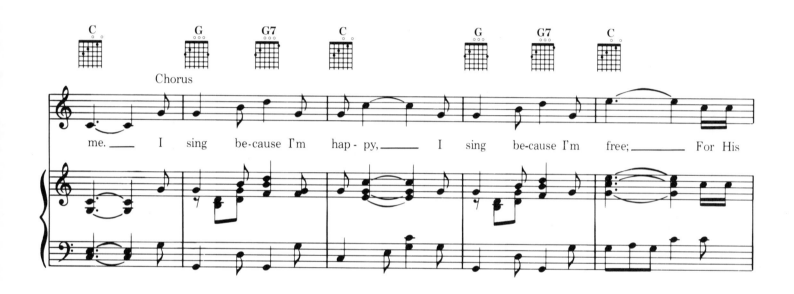

Chorus

me. ___ I sing be-cause I'm hap - py, _____ I sing be-cause I'm free; _____ For His

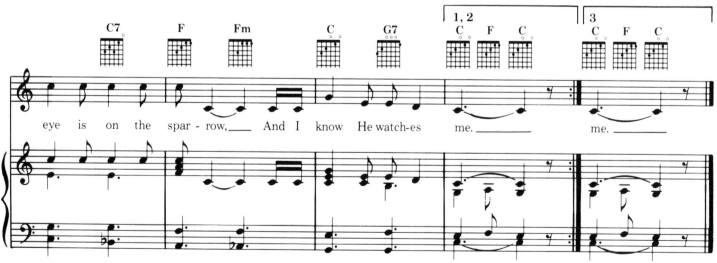

eye is on the spar - row, ___ And I know He watch-es me. _____ me. _____

3. Whenever I am tempted,
Whenever clouds arise.
When song gives place to sighing,
When hope within me dies.
I draw the closer to Him,
From care He sets me free:

HIS NAME IS WONDERFUL

By AUDREY MIEIR

HOLY SPIRIT, THOU ART WELCOME

By DOTTIE RAMBO
and DAVID HUNTSINGER

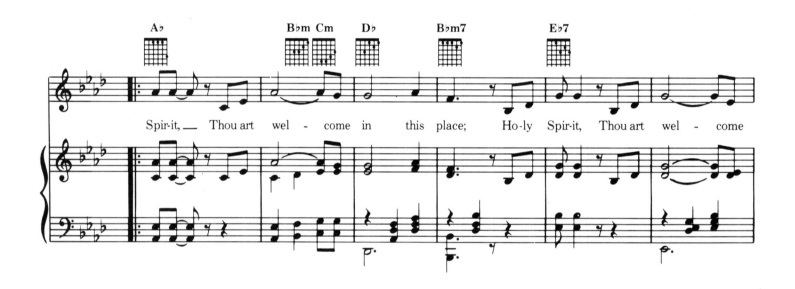

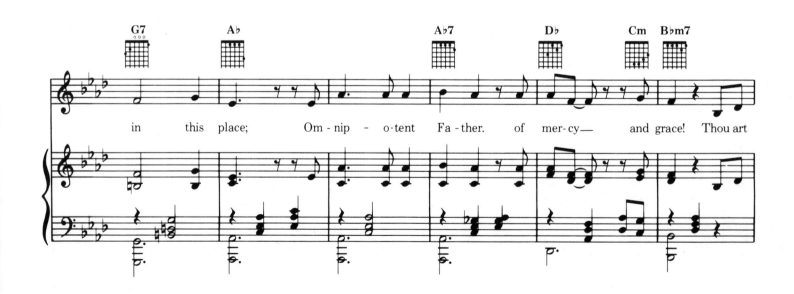

HOME WHERE I BELONG

By PAT TERRY

1. They

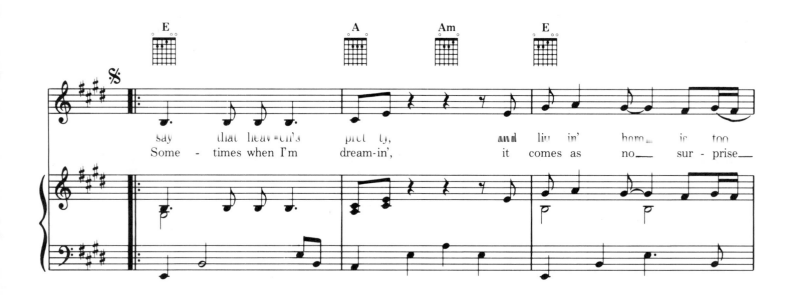

say that heav-en's pret-ty, and liv-in' here is too
Some - times when I'm dream-in', it comes as no__ sur - prise__

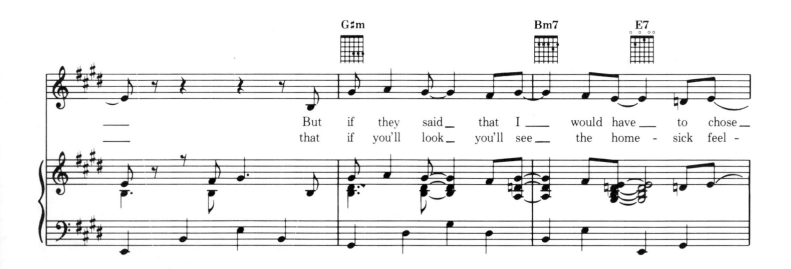

But if they said__ that I __ would have __ to chose __
that if you'll look __ you'll see __ the home - sick feel -

3. When I'm feelin' lonely, and when I'm feelin' blue,
   it's such a joy to know that I am only passin' through.
   I'm headed home, I'm goin' home, where I belong.

HOW GREAT THOU ART

By STUART K. HINE

3. And when I think that God, His Son not sparing,
   Sent Him to die, I scarce can take it in;
   That on the cross, my burden gladly bearing,
   He bled and died to take away my sin;

4. When Christ shall come with shout of acclamation
   And take me home, what joy shall fill my heart!
   Then I shall bow in humble adoration
   And there proclaim, my God, How great Thou art!

I BELIEVE

Words and Music by ERVIN DRAKE,
IRVIN GRAHAM, JIMMY SHIRL and AL STILLMAN

Moderately (with much expression)

I BELIEVE IN YOU

By BUDDY CANNON
and GENE DUNLAP

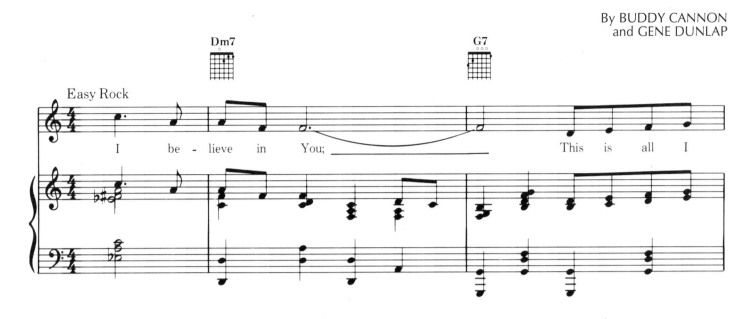

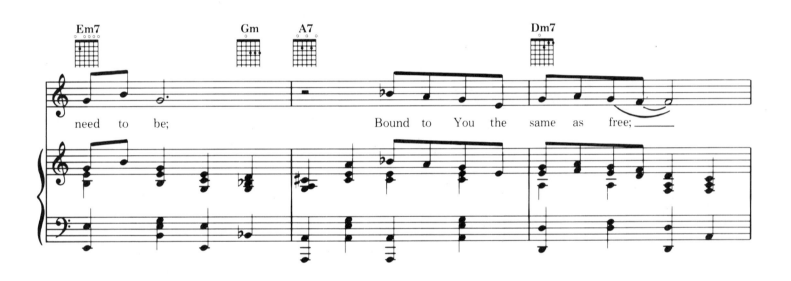

I BOWED ON MY KNEES AND CRIED HOLY

Words by NETTIE DUDLEY WASHINGTON
Music by E.M. DUDLEY CANTWELL

101

I FIND NO FAULT IN HIM

By ANDRAÉ CROUCH

Slowly

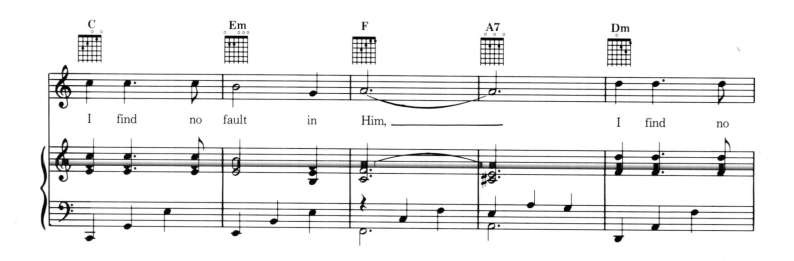

I find no fault in Him, _____ I find no

fault in Him, _____ Yet He was re- ject-ed, de-

I SAW THE LIGHT

Words and Music by
HANK WILLIAMS

I NEVER SHALL FORGET THE DAY

By G.T. SPEER

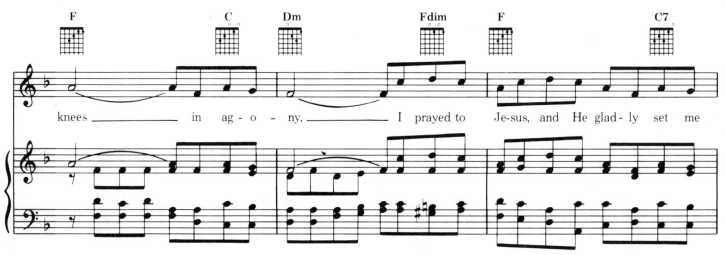

109

2. Now I can feel Him by my side,
   My feeble steps He comes to guide,
   When trials come He comforts me,
   Thru faith in Him,
   O'er sin I have the victory.

3. Oh, sinner, come to Jesus now,
   At his dear feet just humbly bow,
   Confess to Him your ev'ry sin,
   He'll save and cleanse you,
   Give you peace and joy within.

I WANNA BE READY

By AARON BROWN
and GARLAND CRAFT

I WOULD CRAWL ALL THE WAY
(TO THE RIVER)

By CURLY PUTNAM,
DAN WILSON and BUCKY JONES

I'LL FLY AWAY

By ALBERT E. BRUMLEY

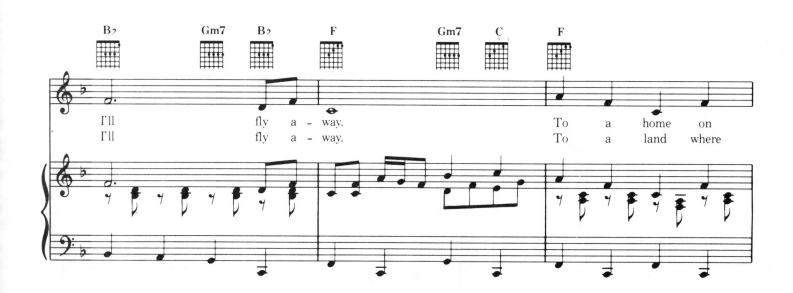

I'M STANDING ON THE SOLID ROCK

By HAROLD LANE

1. Thru my dis-ap-point-ments,
2. E-ven tho' He's gone now,

strife and dis-con-tent-ment, I cast my ev-'ry care on the Lord;
I don't feel a-lone now, With com-fort came the Spir-it of the Lord;

No mat-ter what ob-ses-sion,
Now with His word to guide me,

Pain or deep de-pres-sion, I'm stand-ing on the Sol-id Rock.
From temp-ta-tions hide me, I'm stand-ing on the Sol-id Rock.

Chorus

I'm stand - ing on the

3. Now I'm pressing onward,,
   Each step leads me homeward,
   I'm trusting in my Savior day by day;
   And close is our relation,
   Firm is it's foundation,
   So on this Solid Rock I'll stay.

I'VE BEEN TO CALVARY

By WILLIAM J. GAITHER

I'VE GOT CONFIDENCE

By ANDRAÉ CROUCH

When trou-ble is in ___ my way, ___
Some folks won-der how I smile ___

I can't tell my night ___ from day, ___
E-ven tho' I'm goin' thru trials, ___

When I'm tossed from side to side ___
How ___ can I have a song ___

Like a ship ___ on a rag-ing tide; ___
when ev-'ry-thing is go-in' wrong; ___

I don't wor-ry, I don't fret, ___

IN THE GARDEN

Words and Music by
C. AUSTIN MILES

IN THE SWEET BY AND BY

Traditional

IT TOOK A MIRACLE

Words and Music by
JOHN W. PETERSON

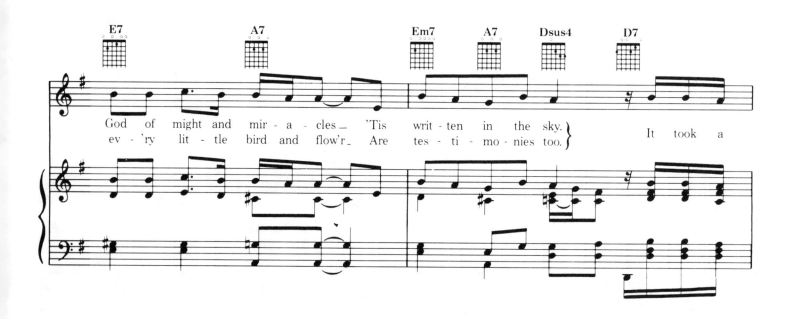

JESUS KNOWS ALL ABOUT IT

By RUSTY GOODMAN

JUST ANY DAY NOW

By AARON WILBURN
and EDDIE CROOK

JUST A CLOSER WALK WITH THEE

Words and Music by
K. MORRIS

3. When my feeble life is o'er,
Time for me will be no more;
On that bright eternal shore
I will walk, dear Lord, close to Thee.

JUST AS I AM

Traditional

Slowly, with movement

KUM BA YAH

Traditional

THE KING IS COMING

Words by WILLIAM J. and GLORIA GAITHER
and CHARLES MILLHUFF
Music by WILLIAM J. GAITHER

THE LIGHTHOUSE

By RONNIE HINSON

Slowly, with expression

There's a light-house ___ on the hill-side that
bod - y that lives a - bout us says,

o - ver - looks life's sea, when I'm tossed ___ it
tear that light - house down, The ___ big ships ___ don't sail this

sends out a light, that I might see; And the
way an - y - more, there's no use of it stand - ing 'round; Then my

LEAD ME, GUIDE ME

Words and Music by
DORIS AKERS

CHORUS-reverently

3. I am lost if You take Your hand from me.

I am blind without Thy Light to see.

Lord, just always let me Thy servant be;

Lead me, oh, Lord, Lead Me.

LOVE WILL ROLL THE CLOUDS AWAY

By HALE REEVES

Gentle Beat

As a-

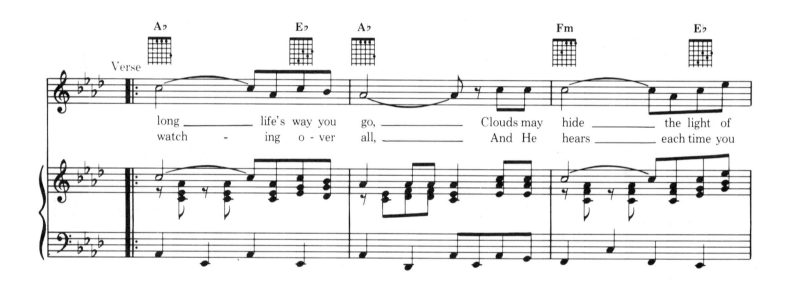

Verse

long _____ life's way you go, _____ Clouds may hide _____ the light of
watch - ing o - ver all, _____ And He hears _____ each time you

day; _____ Have no fear _____ for, friend,_ you
pray; _____ Lift your voice _____ in hap - py

149

LORD, I HOPE THIS DAY IS GOOD

Words and Music by
DAVE HANNER

With Movement

Chorus

Lord,_____ I hope this day is good.__ I'm feel-ing emp-ty and mis-
Lord,_____ have You for-got-ten me?__ I've been pray-in' to You

un - der-stood.__ I should be thank-ful, Lord I know I should,_ But
faith - ful-ly.__ I'm not say-in' I'm a right-eous man,_ But

MANSION OVER THE HILLTOP

Words and Music by
IRA F. STANPHILL

MY GOD IS REAL
(YES, GOD IS REAL)

Words and Music by
KENNETH MORRIS

MY TRIBUTE

Words and Music by
ANDRAÉ CROUCH

161

ME AND JESUS

Words and Music by
TOM T. HALL

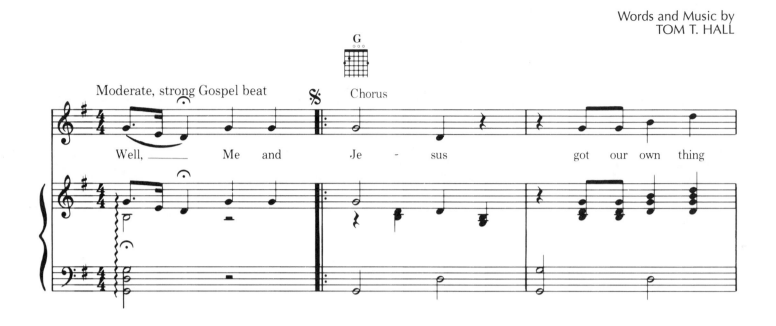

164

3. We can't afford any fancy preachin',
   We can't afford any fancy church;
   We can't afford any fancy singin'
   But you know Jesus got a lot of poor people doin' His work.

THE NIGHT BEFORE EASTER

By DONNIE SUMNER
and DWAYNE FRIEND

Majestically

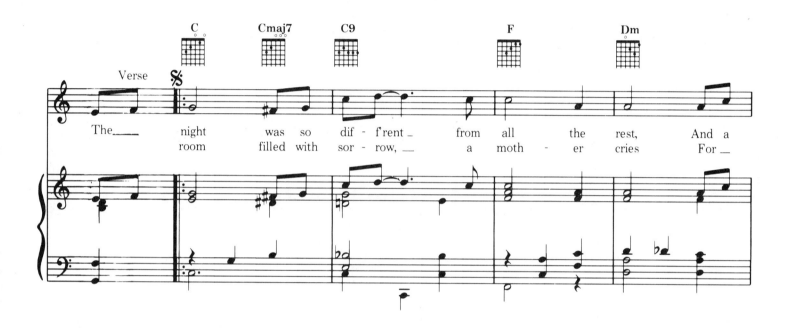

The____ night was so dif - f'rent _ from all the rest, And a
room was filled with sor - row, _ from a moth - er cries For _

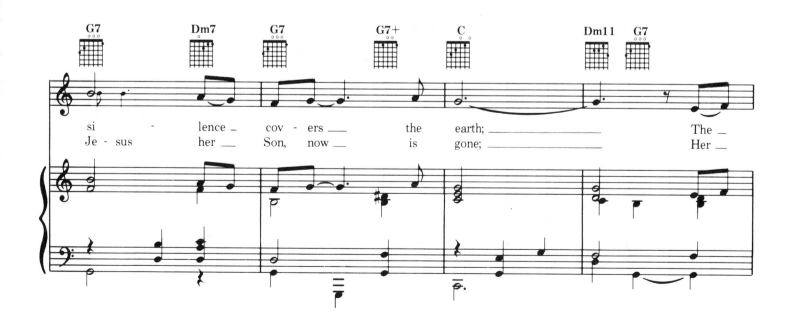

si - lence _ cov - ers __ the earth; _____ The _
Je - sus her _ Son, now _ is gone; _____ Her _

3. At the feet of his mother, a little boy cries,
   Saying "Mama, I don't understand;"
   I remember the look of love in His eyes,
   That I saw by the touch of His hand."

4. The King of all ages, the Giver of life,
   For a moment lies silent and still;
   But a pow'r sent from heaven comes breaking the night,
   And death must bow to His will.

NOW THAT I'VE FOUND YOUR LOVE

Words and Music by
KENT SMITH

3. They will see what Your lasting love can do for me
Now that I found Your love
Time will show that my happiness can only grow
Now that I found Your love.
Your lasting peace is mine to share
by showing others that I care
And show Your joy to all the world around

THE OLD RUGGED CROSS

Moderately Slow

By REV. GEORGE BENNARD

On a hill far a - way stood an old rug-ged cross, The em - blem of
old rug - ged cross I will ev - er be true, Its shame and re -

suf - f'ring and shame; ____ And I love that old cross where the
proach glad - ly bear; ____ Then He'll call me some day to my

dear - est and best For a world of lost sin - ners_ was slain. ____ So I'll
home far a - way, Where His glo - ry for - ev - er_ I'll share. ____

THE OWNER OF THE STORE

Words and Music by ROSEY FITCHPATRICK,
RED LANE and LATHAN

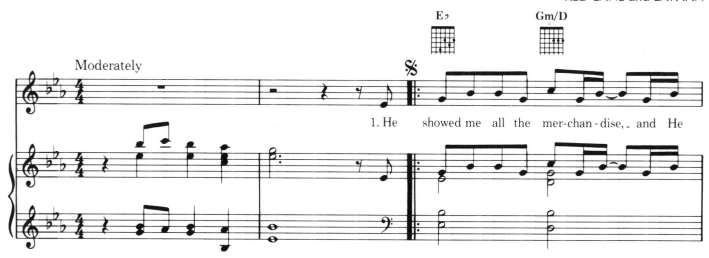

Moderately

1. He showed me all the mer-chan-dise, _ and He

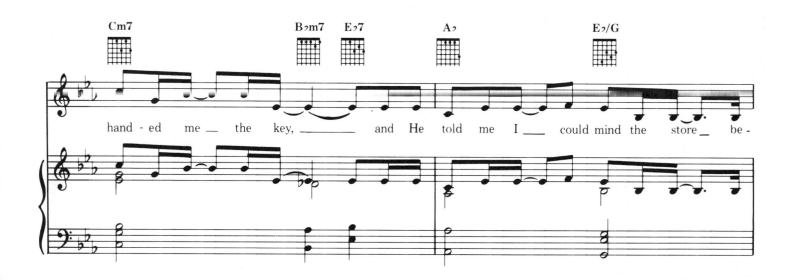

hand-ed me _ the key, _____ and He told me I _ could mind the store _ be-

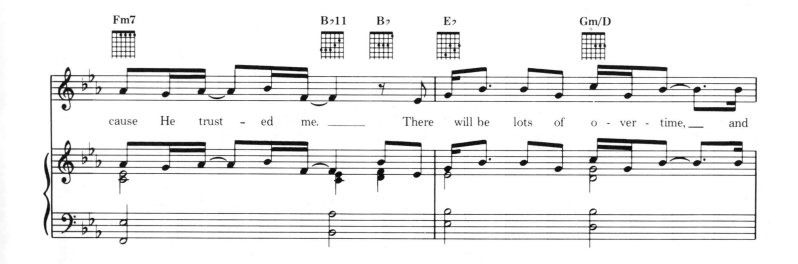

cause He trust-ed me. _____ There will be lots of o-ver-time, _ and

177

2. I'll keep my threshhold open, and help ev'ryone across,
   'Cause he who gives more than receives will never take a loss.
   Keep the owner's image of forgiveness on display,
   He wouldn't want it any other way.

3. Be long on understanding and never shortchange your friends,
   Try to burn the candle of kindness at both ends.
   Keep love for one another piled high upon the rack,
   'cause the owner of the store is coming back.

OVER THE NEXT HILL WE'LL BE HOME

Words and Music by
JOHNNY CASH

2. By the speed that we've been making, I would say there's no mistaking,
   That over the next hill we'll be home;
   There's a place that we are nearing, that so many have been fearing,
   And over the next hill we'll be home.

Chorus:
   When we get there we're all hopin', that we'll find the gate is open,
   And there'll be a refuge from the coming storm;
   For the way's been long and weary, but at last the end is nearing,
   And over the next hill we'll be home.

THE PILGRIM

By HONEYTREE

(THERE'LL BE)
PEACE IN THE VALLEY
(FOR ME)

Words and Music by
THOMAS A. DORSEY

3. There the bear will be gentle, the wolf will be tame,
   And the lion will lay down by the lamb,
   The host from the wild will be led by a Child,
   I'll be changed from the creature I am.

4. No headaches or heartaches or misunderstands,
   No confusion or trouble won't be,
   No frowns to defile, just a long endless smile,
   There'll be peace and contentment for me.

PRECIOUS LORD, TAKE MY HAND

(a/k/a TAKE MY HAND, PRECIOUS LORD)

Words and Music by
THOMAS A. DORSEY

Slow with Spirit

PUT YOUR HAND IN THE HAND

Words and Music by
GENE MacLELLAN

190

PRECIOUS MEMORIES

Traditional Spiritual

3. As I travel on life's pathway, I know not what life shall hold;
   As I wander hopes grow fonder, Precious mem'ries flood my soul.

RISE AGAIN

By DALLAS HOLM

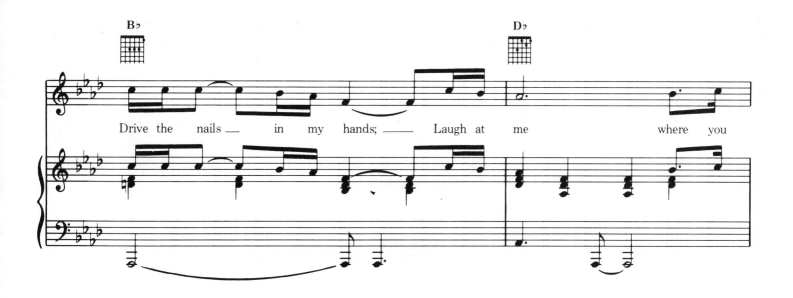

196

2. Go ahead, and mock my name; My love for you is still the same;
   Go ahead and bury me; But very soon I will be free!
   'Cause I'll . . . (*chorus*)

3. Go ahead and say I'm dead and gone, But you will see that you were wrong
   Go ahead, try to hide the Son, But all will see that I'm the One!
   'Cause I'll . . . (*chorus*)

ROOM AT THE CROSS FOR YOU

By IRA F. STANPHILL

With feeling

ROCK OF AGES

Traditional

3. While I draw this fleeting breath
When my eyes shall close in death
When I rise to worlds unknown
And behold Thee on Thy throne
Rock of Ages cleft for me
Let me hide myself in Thee.

SWEET, SWEET SPIRIT

By DORIS AKERS

There's a sweet, sweet Spir - it in this

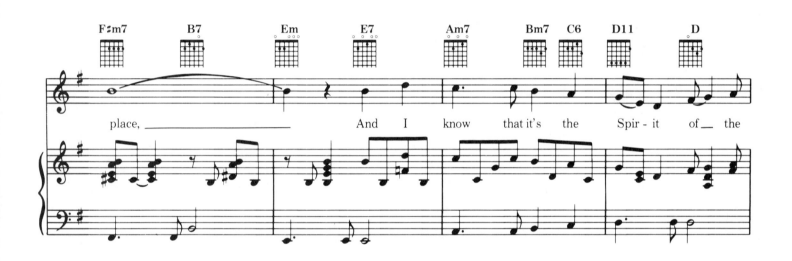

place, _____ And I know that it's the Spir - it of __ the

Lord. _____ There are sweet ex - pres - sions on each

202

SATAN, YOU'RE A LIAR

By AARON WILBURN

With confidence

Verse

You said I'd nev-er make it, you
gave my heart to Je-sus you

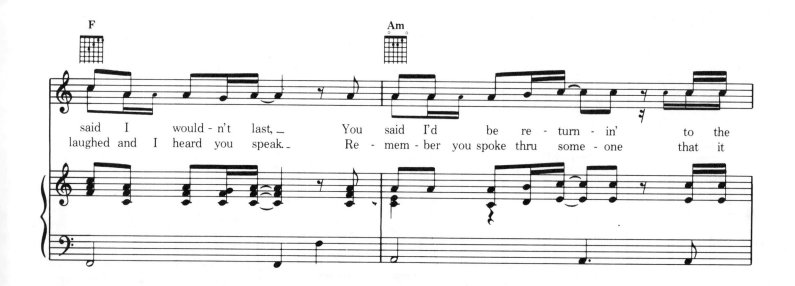

said I would-n't last, ___ You said I'd be re-turn-in' to the
laughed and I heard you speak. ___ Re-mem-ber you spoke thru some-one that it

3. I know you're everything in this world except my friend,
   But still you have the courage, the nerve to come around again.
   You tell me I'm not born again, Heaven's not reality,
   That Jesus Christ is not the Song of God, Satan, listen good to me.

SAY I DO

By RAY HILDEBRAND

Moderate tempo

An-y-bod-y here want-a live for-ev-er, Say "I

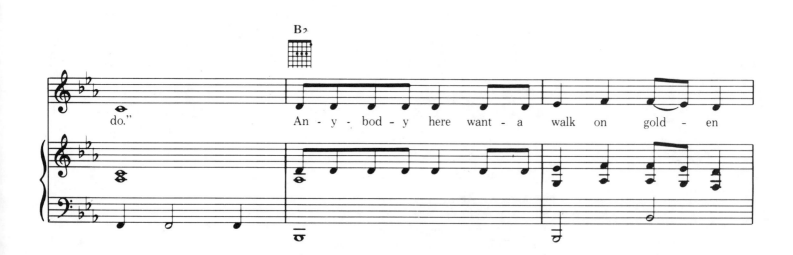

do." An-y-bod-y here want-a walk on gold-en

SINCE JESUS CAME INTO MY HEART

Words by R.H. McDANIEL
Music by CHARLES H. GABRIEL

SINCERELY YOURS

By GARY CHAPMAN

Lord, I take my pen to write to You a letter, Know-ing

e-ven now You know what's on my mind; But I think per-haps it might make me feel

213

SING YOUR PRAISE TO THE LORD

Words and Music by
RICHARD MULLINS

sing, sing,___ sing,   let me hear ya now, sing, sing,___ sing.___

SPECIAL DELIVERY

By RON and CAROL HARRIS

Nev - er was an - y - one like Him,
Where He went love was there al - so,

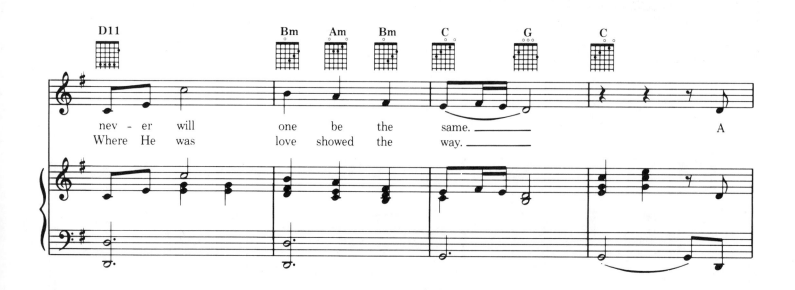

nev - er will one be the same. _____
Where He was love showed the way. _____ A

THE SUN'S COMING UP

By DEE GASKIN

THERE'S SOMETHING
ABOUT THAT NAME

Words by WILLIAM J. and GLORIA GAITHER
Music by WILLIAM J. GAITHER

RECITATON

1. Jesus, the mere mention of His Name can calm the storm, heal the broken, raise the dead. At the Name of Jesus, I've seen sin-hardened men melted, derelicts transformed, the lights of hope put back into the eyes of a hopeless child. . .

At the Name of Jesus, hatred and bitterness turned to love and forgiveness, arguments cease.

I've heard a mother softly breathe His Name at the bedside of a child delirious from fever, and I've watched that little body grow quiet and the fevered brow cool.

I've sat beside a dying saint, her body racked with pain, who in those final fleeting seconds summoned her last ounce of ebbing strength to whisper earth's sweetest Name - Jesus, Jesus. . .

2. Emperors have tried to destroy it; philosophies have tried to stamp it out. Tyrants have tried to wash it from the face of the earth with the very blood of those who claimed it. Yet still it stands.

And there shall be that final day when every voice that has ever uttered a sound - every voice of Adam's race shall raise in one great mighty chorus to proclaim the Name of Jesus - for in that day "Every knee shall bow and every tongue shall confess that Jesus Chirst is Lord!!!"

Ah - so you see - it was not mere chance that caused the angel one night long ago to say to a virgin maiden, "His Name shall be called Jesus." Jesus - Jesus - Jesus. You know, there is something about that Name. . .

THROUGH IT ALL

By ANDRAÉ CROUCH

2. I've been to lots of places
   And I've seen a lot of faces
   There've been times I've felt so all alone,
   But in my lonely hour,
   yes those precious lonely hours
   Jesus let me know I was His own. *(chorus)*

3. I thank God for the mountains
   And I thank Him for the valleys,
   I thank Him for the storms
   He brought me through,
   For if I'd never had a problem
   I wouldn't know that He could solve them
   I'd never know what faith in God could do. *(chorus)*

TURN! TURN! TURN!
(TO EVERYTHING THERE IS A SEASON)

Words from the Book of Ecclesiastes
Adaptation and Music by PETE SEEGER

TURN YOUR RADIO ON

Words and Music by
ALBERT E. BRUMLEY

Well, come and lis-ten in to a ra-di-o sta-tion where the might-y
bod-y has a ra-di-o re-ceiv-er, all you got to

hosts of heav-en sing, Turn your ra-di-o on, Turn your ra-di-o
do is lis-ten for the call, Turn your ra-di-o on, Turn your ra-di-o

on. If you want to feel those good vi-
on. If you lis-ten in you will be a be-

VICTORY IN JESUS

By E.M. BARTLETT

WAYFARING STRANGER

Traditional American Folksong

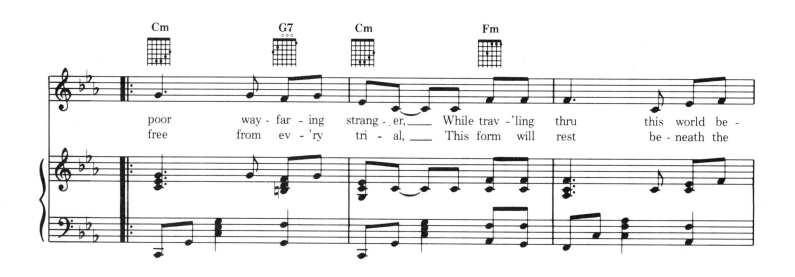

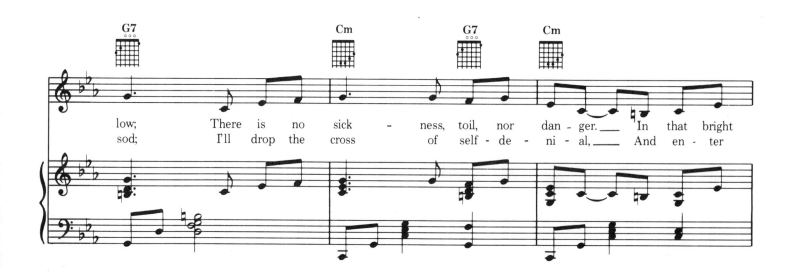

WE SHALL BEHOLD HIM

Words and Music by
DOTTIE RAMBO

248

WHAT A BEAUTIFUL DAY
(FOR THE LORD TO COME AGAIN)

By AARON WILBURN
and EDDIE CROOK

251

WHEN THE ROLL IS CALLED UP YONDER

Words and Music by
JAMES M. BLACK

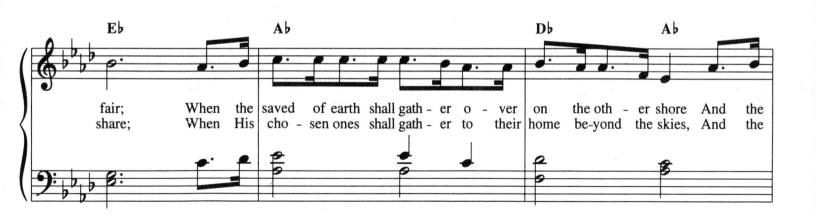

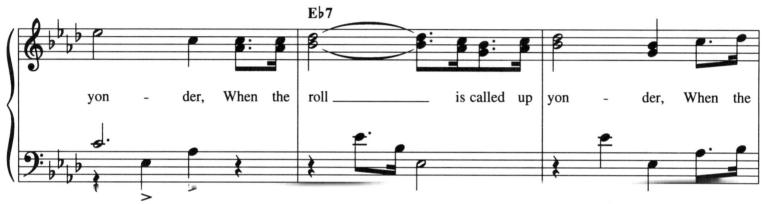

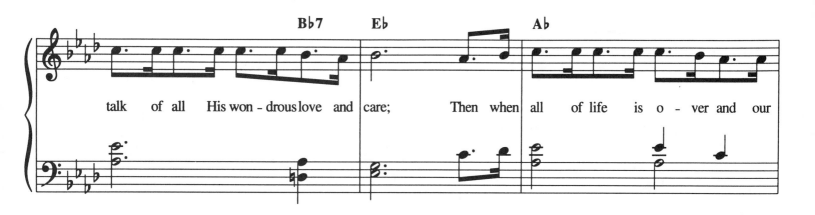

talk of all His won- drous love and care; Then when all of life is o - ver and our

work on earth is done And the roll is called up yon - der, I'll be there! When the

roll _____ is called up yon - der, When the roll _____ is called up yon - der, When the

roll _____ is called up yon - der, When the roll is called up yon - der, I'll be there!

WHAT A DAY THAT WILL BE

By JIM HILL

WHISPERING HOPE

Words and Music by
ALICE HAWTHORNE

WHO AM I

By RUSTY GOODMAN

WHY ME?
(a/k/a WHY ME, LORD?)

Words and Music by
KRIS KRISTOFFERSON

Moderately, with a Gospel feeling

Why me, Lord?
What have I ev-er done to de-serve e-ven

If you think there's a way I can try to re-

one of the pleas-ures I've known? Tell me, Lord, What did I ev-er

pay all I've tak-en from you, May-be, Lord, I can show some-one

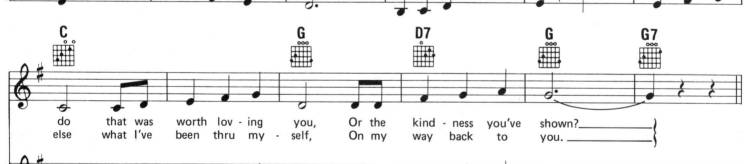

do that was worth lov-ing you, Or the kind-ness you've shown?

else what I've been thru my-self, On my way back to you.

WILL THE CIRCLE BE UNBROKEN

Words by ADA R. HABERSHON
Music by CHARLES H. GABRIEL

WINGS OF A DOVE

Words and Music by
BOB FERGUSON

3. When Jesus went down to the waters that day,
   He was baptized in the usual way.
   When it was done, God blessed His Son.
   He sent him His love On the wings of a dove.

WITHOUT HIM

By MYLON R. LeFEVRE

Without Him I could do nothing, _____ Without Him I would be dying, _____ With-

out Him I'd sure-ly fail; _____ Without Him I'd be en-slaved; _____ With-

out Him I would be drift-ing _____ Like a ship without Him life would be hope-less _____ But with Je-sus, thank

YOU BRING OUT THE LOVE IN ME

Words and Music by KENT BLAZY
and KEITH FREEMAN

I'd giv - en

up - on my heart 'til You came a - long And
You gave my soul a new love song to sing I

me. Now I can share what

I feel in - side; There's so much to live for and

noth - ing to hide; _____ You

love in me. _____

YOU MAKE IT RAIN FOR ME

Words and Music by
LARRY STALLINGS

YOU NEEDED ME

Words and Music by
RANDY GOODRUM

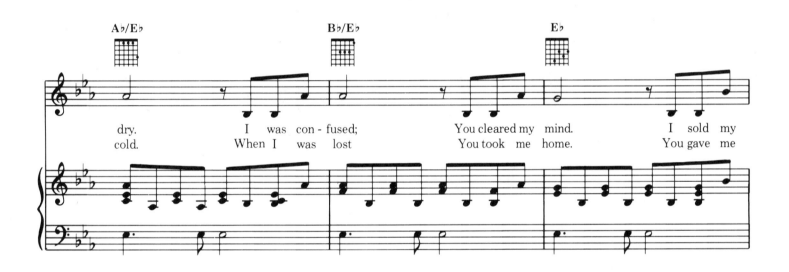

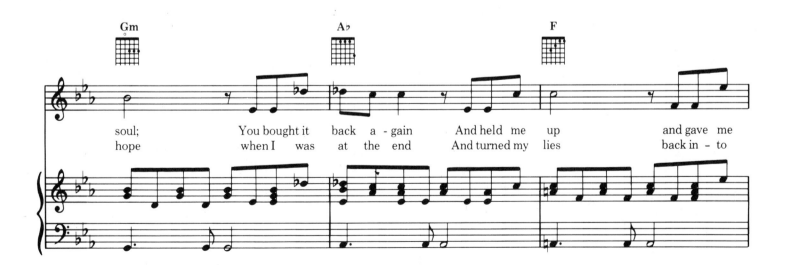

THE ULTIMATE SERIES

This comprehensive series features jumbo collections of piano/vocal arrangements with guitar chords. Each volume features an outstanding selection of your favorite songs. Collect them all for the ultimate music library!

Treasury Of Standards Volume 1

A must-have collection of 100 of the greatest standards of all-time from A-I featuring: All The Things You Are • Bewitched • Bluesette • Don't Cry For Me Argentina • A Fine Romance • From This Moment On • Gonna Build A Mountain • Heartlight • I Can't Get Started • and more!

00361431 . . . . $17.95

Treasury Of Standards Volume 2

Volume 2 in a collection of 100 favorite standards from I-O featuring: I'll Never Smile Again • If I Loved You • It's Not Unusual • Just A Gigolo • The Last Time I Saw Paris • Look For The Silver Lining • Make Believe • Misty • One Note Samba • Our Day Will Come • and more!

00361433 . . . . $17.95

Treasury Of Standards Volume 3

The last in a 3-volume set, features 100 best-loved standards from P-Z including: People • Satin Doll • Smoke Gets In Your Eyes • Strangers In The Night • Sunrise, Sunset • That's All • Watch What Happens • Who Can I Turn To • You Don't Bring Me Flowers.

00361435 . . . . $17.95

All-Time Hits – 100 Favorite Standards

A super song selection, including: After You've Gone • Bugle Call Rag • The Christmas Song (Chestnuts Roasting On An Open Fire) • Drifting And Dreaming • Easy Street • Flamingo • Hello, Dolly! • If He Walked Into My Life • Ivory Tower • The Man That Got Away • Moonlight Bay • Notre Dame Victory March • Sentimental Journey • Sioux City Sue • Tenderly • Unchained Melody • We Need A Little Christmas • What I Did For Love • You Call Everybody Darling • more.

00361424 . . . . $17.95

Broadway Gold

100 show tunes from a wide variety of Broadway's biggest hits: Bess, You Is My Woman • Happy Talk • I Love Paris • The Lady Is A Tramp • Let Me Entertain You • Memory • My Funny Valentine • Oklahoma • The Rain In Spain • Some Enchanted Evening • When I Fall In Love • It Only Takes A Moment • Mame • Seventy-Six Trombones • Summer Nights • Till There Was You • Tomorrow • What I Did For Love • Silk Stockings • many more.

00361396 . . . . $17.95

Broadway Platinum

A collection of 100 popular Broadway show tunes, featuring the hits: As Long As He Needs Me • Bali Ha'i • Beauty And The Beast • Camelot • Consider Yourself • Everything's Coming Up Roses • Getting To Know You • Gigi • Do You Hear The People Sing • Hello, Young Lovers • I'll Be Seeing You • If Ever I Would Leave You • My Favorite Things • On A Clear Day • People • September Song • She Loves Me • Sun And Moon • Try To Remember • Younger Than Springtime • Who Can I Turn To • many more.

00311496 . . . . $19.95

Christmas

100 of the best-loved traditional and contemporary songs of the season, including: Away In A Manger • The First Noel • Hark! The Herald Angels Sing • The Holly And The Ivy • I Heard The Bells On Christmas Day • Jingle Bells • Joy To The World • Let It Snow! Let It Snow! Let It Snow! • Mary's Little Boy Child • My Favorite Things • Nuttin' For Christmas • O Holy Night • Rudolph, The Red-Nosed Reindeer • Silent Night • Sleigh Ride • Still, Still, Still • Toyland • We Three Kings Of Orient Are • We Wish You A Merry Christmas • and more.

00361399 . . . . $17.95

Contemporary – 60 Solid Gold Hits

60 contemporary smash hits, including: Candle In The Wind • Don't Know Much • Don't Worry, Be Happy • Faith • I Write The Songs • I'll Be Loving You (Forever) • Islands In The Stream • Kokomo • Lost In Your Eyes • Memory • Sailing • Somewhere Out There • We Didn't Start The Fire • With Or Without You • You Needed Me • much more!

00490289 . . . . $17.95

Country

Over 90 of your favorite country hits in one collection! Features: Achy Breaky Heart • Act Naturally • Always On My Mind • American Made • Boot Scootin' Boogie • Brand New Man • Crazy • Down At The Twist And Shout • Folsom Prison Blues • Hey, Good Lookin' • Lucille • Neon Moon • Southern Nights • Where've You Been • and more.

00310036 . . . . $19.95

Gospel

100 of the most inspirational gospel songs ever compiled, featuring: Because He Lives • Climb Ev'ry Mountain • Daddy Sang Bass • El Shaddai • He • He Touched Me • His Eye Is On The Sparrow • How Great Thou Art • I Never Shall Forget The Day • I Saw The Light • I Would Crawl All The Way To The River • Just A Closer Walk With Thee • Just Any Day Now • Kum Ba Yah • Lead Me, Guide Me • Peace In The Valley • Rock Of Ages • Sincerely Yours • The Sun's Coming Up • Take My Hand, Precious Lord • What A Beautiful Day • Wings Of A Dove • more.

00241009 . . . . $17.95

Rock 'N' Roll

100 of the biggest rock 'n' roll hits from 1954-1965: All Shook Up • At The Hop • Blue Suede Shoes • Bye Bye, Love • Chantilly Lace • Diana • Hello, Mary Lou (Goodbye Heart) • I Want To Hold Your Hand • It's My Party • Lollipop • Peggy Sue • Put Your Head On My Shoulder • Save The Last Dance For Me • Sixteen Candles • Surfin' U.S.A. • That'll Be The Day • True Love Ways • Wake Up, Little Susie • What's Your Name? • more.

00361411 . . . . $17.95

Singalong!

100 of the best-loved popular songs ever: Ain't Misbehavin' • All Of Me • Beer Barrel Polka • California, Here I Come • The Candy Man • Crying In The Chapel • Edelweiss • Feelings • Five Foot Two, Eyes Of Blue • For Me And My Gal • Goodnight Irene • I Left My Heart In San Francisco • Indiana • It's A Small World • It's Hard To Be Humble • Mickey Mouse March • Que Sera, Sera • This Land Is Your Land • Too Fat Polka • When Irish Eyes Are Smiling • and more.

00361418 . . . . $17.95

Jazz Standards

100 great jazz selections, featuring: Ain't Misbehavin' • All Of Me • Bernie's Tune • Early Autumn • A Foggy Day • From This Moment On • Here's That Rainy Day • I've Got You Under My Skin • Manhattan • Meditation • Moonlight In Vermont • My Funny Valentine • Route 66 • A Taste Of Honey • There's A Small Hotel • What A Difference A Day Made • You'd Be So Nice To Come Home To.

00361407 . . . . $17.95

Love And Wedding Songbook

90 songs of devotion including: The Anniversary Waltz • Canon In D • Endless Love • For All We Know • Forever And Ever, Amen • Just The Way You Are • Longer • The Lord's Prayer • Love Me Tender • One Hand, One Heart • Somewhere • Sunrise, Sunset • Through The Years • Trumpet Voluntary • and many, many more!

00361445 . . . . $17.95

Standards, Vol. 1 – 100 All-Time Favorites

Volume 1 of a 3-volume set includes classic favorite songs from A-I, featuring: Ain't Misbehavin' • Blueberry Hill • Careless • Climb Ev'ry Mountain • Edelweiss • A Foggy Day • Georgy Girl • Here's That Rainy Day • I Remember It Well • I'm Beginning To See The Light • many more.

00361421 . . . . $17.95

Standards, Vol. 2 – 100 All-Time Favorites

More favorite titles from I-S, including: The Lady Is A Tramp • Let Me Call You Sweetheart • Let's Get Away From It All • Lost In The Stars • Love Me Tender • Moonlight And Roses • My Favorite Things • My Heart Belongs To Me • Never On Sunday • Nice Work If You Can Get It • The Object Of My Affection • Opus One • Pennies From Heaven • more.

00361422 . . . . $17.95

Standards, Vol. 3 – 100 All-Time Favorites

The last of the three-volume set features favorite titles S-Y: September Song • Smile • Songbird • What Kind Of Fool Am I ? • The Sound Of Music • This Is All I Ask • A Walk In The Black Forest • more

00361423 . . . . $17.95

FOR MORE INFORMATION, SEE YOUR LOCAL MUSIC DEALER, OR WRITE TO:

HAL•LEONARD™ CORPORATION
7777 W. BLUEMOUND RD. P.O. BOX 13819 MILWAUKEE, WI 53213

Prices, contents, and availability subject to change without notice. Availability and pricing may vary outside the U.S.A.

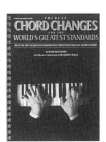